Watch it Grow

Life Cycles

Siân Smith

Raintree

www.raintreepublishers.co.uk
Visit our website to find out more information about Raintree books.

To order:
☎ Phone 0845 6044371
🖷 Fax +44 (0) 1865 312263
🖂 Email myorders@raintreepublishers.co.uk

Customers from outside the UK please telephone +44 1865 312262

Raintree is an imprint of Capstone Global Library Limited, a company incorporated in England and Wales having its registered office at 7 Pilgrim Street, London, EC4V 6LB – Registered company number: 6695582

Edited by Daniel Nunn, Rebecca Rissman, and Harriet Milles
Designed by Joanna Hinton-Malivoire
Picture research by Mica Brancic
Originated by Capstone Global Library Ltd.
Production by Victoria Fitzgerald
Printed and bound in China by Leo Paper Products Ltd

ISBN 978 1 406 22897 7 (hardback)
15 14 13 12 11
10 9 8 7 6 5 4 3 2 1

ISBN 978 1 406 22968 4 (paperback)
16 15 14 13 12
10 9 8 7 6 5 4 3 2 1

British Library Cataloguing in Publication Data
Smith, Sian.
  Life cycles. – (Acorn plus)
  1. Life cycles (Biology)–Pictorial works–Juvenile
  literature.
  I. Title II. Series
  571.8-dc22
A full catalogue record for this book is available from the British Library.

Acknowledgements
We would like to thank the following for permission to reproduce photographs: Photolibrary p. 16 (Animals Animals/Zigmund Leszczynski); Shutterstock **pp. 4 bottom left** (© Antos777), **4 bottom middle** (© Natalie Jean), **4 bottom right** (© Geanina Bechea), **4 top left** (© B. Stefanov), **4 top middle** (© Stephanie Barbary), **4 top right** (© Trucic), **5 top left** (© Joy Brown), **5 top right** (© Outsider), **5 bottom left** (© Alexnika), **5 bottom right** (© Natalia Yudenich), **6** (© Bluerain), **7** (© Bogdan Wankowicz), **8** (© S-eyerkaufer), **9 left** (© Triff), **9 right** (© Jan Zoetekouw), **10** (© Stargazer), **11 top left** (© Orionmystery@flickr), **11 top right** (© Yellowj), **11 bottom left** (© Ann Worthy), **11 bottom right** (© Eric Isselée), **12** (© Seleznev Valery), **13** (© Koshevnyk), **14** (© Greg Henry), **15** (© Alexander Chelmodeev), **17** (© Cathy Keifer), **18** (© Petrov Anton), **19 top left** (© Splash), **19 top right** (© Jan van der Hoeven), **19 bottom left** (© Torsten Dietrich), **19 bottom right** (© Dr. Morley Read, **20 top left** (© Melissa King), **20 top right** (© Ivan Pavlisko), **20 bottom left** (© Privilege), **20 bottom middle & bottom right** (© Yuri Arcurs), **21 left** (© rSnapshotPhotos), **21 right** (© Monkey Business Images), **22 top left** (© Marta P.), **22 top middle** (© Leolintang), **22 top right** (© Shane W Thompson), **22 bottom left** (© Olga Lipatova), **22 bottom middle** (© Pichugin Dmitry), **22 bottom right** (© Liew Weng Keong).

Cover photograph of a grandfather and granddaughter reproduced with permission of Photolibrary (Stockbroker).

We would like to thank Michael Bright for his invaluable help in the preparation of this book.

Every effort has been made to contact copyright holders of any material reproduced in this book. Any omissions will be rectified in subsequent printings if notice is given to the publisher.

Contents

What is a life cycle? 4

Life begins 6

Growing up 8

Making new life 10

Dying 14

Unusual life cycles 16

The human life cycle 20

How long is one life cycle? 22

Words to know 23

Index 24

Notes for parents and teachers 24

Some words appear in bold, **like this**. You can find out what they mean in "Words to know" on page 23.

What is a life cycle?

There are lots of different types of living things. All animals such as birds, insects, and people are living things. All plants are living things, too. All living things have a life cycle.

A life cycle shows the changes or different **stages** that a living thing goes through in its life. These changes follow a **pattern**. They happen in the same order for each living thing.

Life begins

The main **stages** in a life cycle are the same for all living things. The start of a life cycle is when life begins. An animal life cycle might start with an egg or a baby.

first leaves

shoot

seed

root

For most plants, life begins with a seed. When a seed has water and sunlight, it can begin to grow into a plant.

Growing up

Baby animals grow up to become adults who can look after themselves. Animals and plants go through lots of different changes before they become adults.

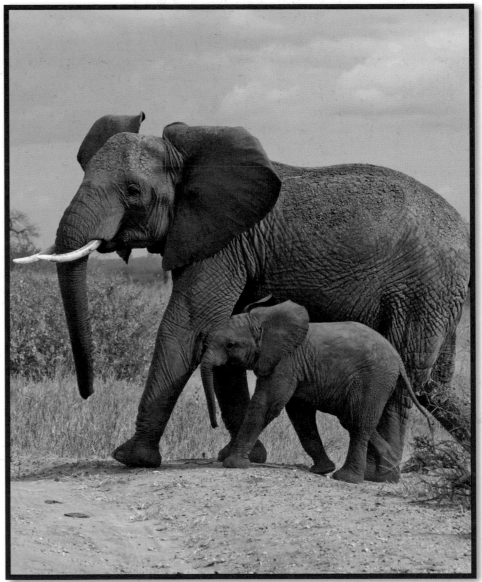

Some living things take a long time to grow up.
Others grow up quickly. A sunflower seed can grow
into a fully grown plant in about 12 weeks. It takes
an elephant many years to become an adult.

Making new life

When animals become adults they can create new life by making babies. This is called **reproduction**. Plants make new plants by reproducing, too.

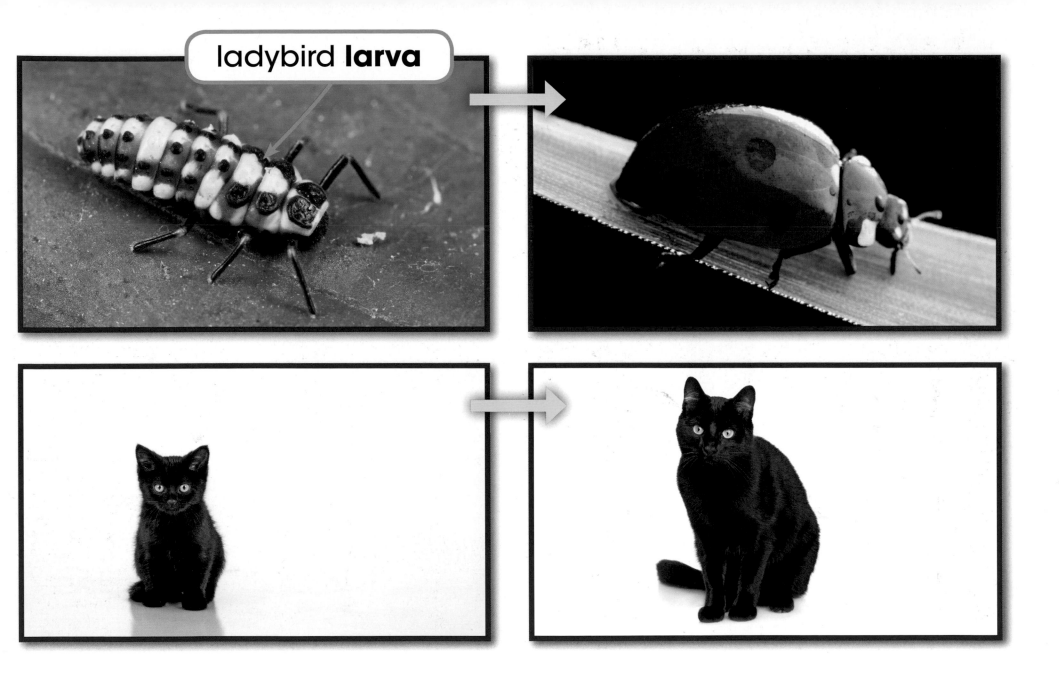

ladybird **larva**

Some animals start life inside their mother's body. Some animals start life in eggs. Some baby animals look very different from their parents at first. Others look just like their parents.

11

pollen

Most plants make new life with seeds. To make a seed, **pollen** has to get from one part of a flower to another. Pollen can be carried by the wind, or by insects, birds, and bats.

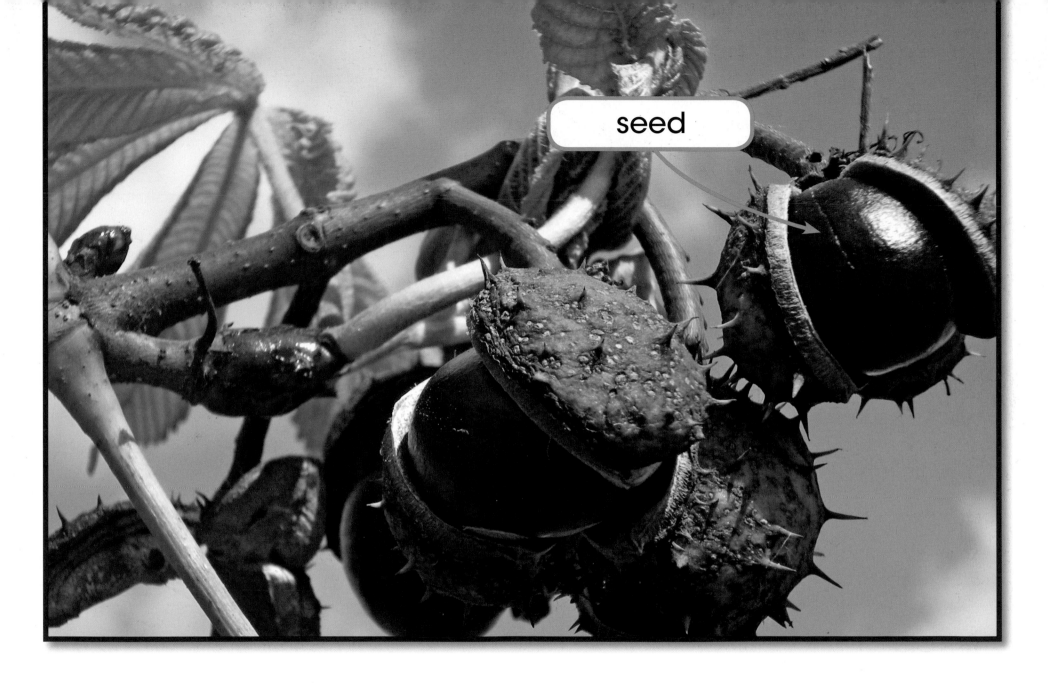

seed

Once a flower has the pollen it needs, a seed starts to grow inside the flower. Seeds have cases around them to keep them safe. Inside each seed is the start of a new plant.

Dying

Nothing that is living can stay alive forever. After time, all living things will get old and die. This is part of the life cycle, too.

young tree

Dying is the last **stage** in a life cycle. But life cycles go on because animals make babies and plants make seeds. This starts the life cycle all over again.

Unusual life cycles

old skin

Many animals go through amazing changes
to become adults. Some animals grow new skin.
They lose their old skin as they grow up. This is
called **moulting**.

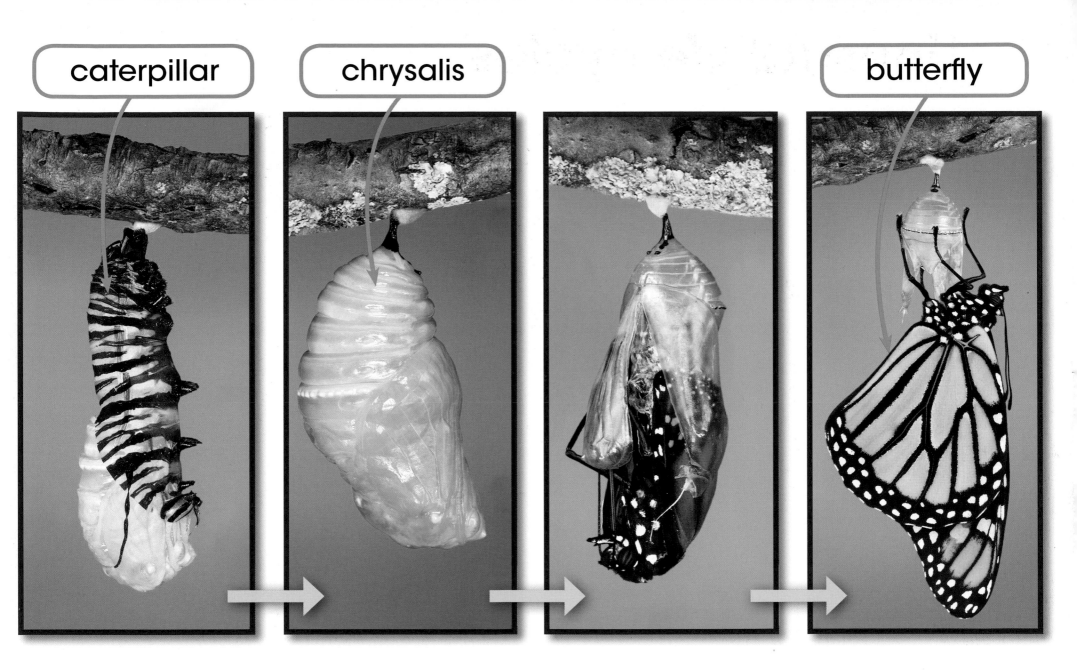

Some insects change completely when they turn into adults. A butterfly starts life as a caterpillar. It spins a cover around its body, called a **chrysalis**. Inside the chrysalis it changes into an adult!

frog

Another special group of animals are called **amphibians**. Amphibians are animals such as frogs, toads, and newts. They are born in water, but they spend most of their lives on land.

Amphibians lay their eggs in water. The young have **gills** so they can breathe underwater, and tails to help them swim. As they grow, they get **lungs** to breathe in air, and legs for moving on land.

The human life cycle

Humans have life cycles, too. A baby becomes a child. A child becomes a teenager, and then an adult. Adults get older, and eventually they die. When adults have babies, they start the life cycle all over again.

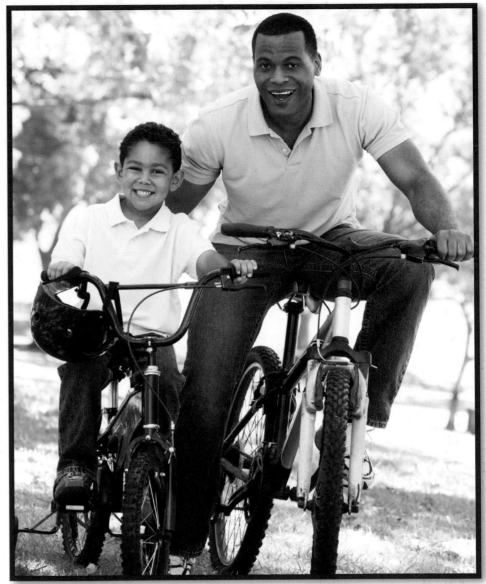

As we grow, our bodies do not change on the outside as much as butterflies or frogs do. Humans take care of their young and teach them new things for much longer than other animals.

How long is one life cycle?

olive tree

human

sea lion

marigold

hippopotamus

mayfly

How long do you think the living things in the photos might live for?

Answers on page 23

Words to know

amphibian type of animal that can live in water or on land

chrysalis case around an insect. Inside a chrysalis, an insect changes into an adult.

gills part of an animal's body that helps it to breathe underwater

larva young insect

lung part of an animal's body that helps it to breathe in air

moulting growing new skin and losing the old skin

pattern happening in the same order

pollen powder made by plants. Plants reproduce by using pollen.

reproduction to make new life

stage one part or section of a life cycle

Answers to quiz on page 22:
olive tree about 500 to 900 years
human about 70 to 80 years
sea lion about 17 years
marigold about 1 year
hippopotamus about 45 years
mayfly about 30 minutes to 1 day

Index

animals 4, 6, 8, 10–11, 12, 15, 16, 18, 21

baby 6, 11, 20

birds 4, 12

changes 4, 8, 16–17, 21

eggs 6, 11, 19

humans 20–21, 22

insects 4, 12, 16–17

plants 4, 7, 8, 10, 12, 15

seed 7, 9, 12–13, 15

Notes for parents and teachers

Before reading

Show the children the front cover of the book. Ask them what they think life cycle means. Explain to the children that a life cycle shows the changes or different stages a living thing goes through in its life.

After reading

- Depending on the time of year, ask each child to create a book about a living thing's life cycle. For example, if it is autumn, ask them to make a story about the life cycle of an apple tree. Each page can show one stage of the living thing's life cycle.
- Cut out pictures of different stages of a life cycle. Ask children to order and name the stages. Stick the pictures or photos in the correct order on a display chart.
- As an on-going class activity, plant a fast growing seed of a plant that also produces seeds quickly (for example, a bean). Encourage the children to observe the changes and stages of its life cycle week by week.